CW00739783

A Dalesman's War

Carole Morland

HAYLOFT PUBLISHING LTD

First published 2010

Hayloft Publishing Ltd, South Stainmore,
Kirkby Stephen, Cumbria, CA17 4DJ

tel: 07971 352473
email: books@hayloft.eu
web: www.hayloft.eu

ISBN 1 904524 78 8

CAP data for this title are available from the British Library

Designed, printed and bound in the EU

Papers used by Hayloft are natural, recyclable products made from wood grown in
sustainable forest. The manufacturing processes conform to the environmental
regulations of the country of origin.

To Doris

Foreword

I was deeply touched to be asked by Carole to write a brief foreword for her book which follows the fortunes of her father Stan Haygarth through his childhood, war-time service and life after the Second World War, both in Dent and Sedbergh.

Carole knew that, as a former officer, both in the Parachute Regiment and the Coldstream Guards for over 30 years, I would understand the plight of her father who was horrifically burned in France when his tank was shot up by German Panzers in an ambush and set alight. As a consequence of his injuries, Stan had to spend many months in various hospitals having skin grafts and amputations of various fingers all of which was incredibly painful.

Stan's physical injuries were relatively straight forward compared to the mental anguish that he clearly suffered for the remainder of his life. Post Traumatic Stress (PTS) as it is now known, is still little understood even to this day and a condition that the MOD is now, at long last, having to recognise and take more seriously. At the time of Stan's injuries the treatment for PTS was virtually non-existent and was better known as 'shell shock', a rather old-fashioned World War One term.

When I was a young Platoon Commander in the First Battalion the Parachute Regiment, recently commissioned, the battalion was sent to Aden in 1967 to help to ensure the orderly withdrawal of British Forces in what is now Yemen on the Saudi Arabian peninsula. Life then was very much an adventure and one felt invincible. This was soon to change as heavy fighting with the insurgents in and around Sheik Ottoman resulted in many casualties. I sadly lost one of the young soldiers, who died alongside me shot through the head, and a number of my soldiers were injured, some more seriously than others.

We were all young men under 22 years of age forced to grow up very quickly and adjust to the realities of life fighting a limited war in inhospitable country thousands of miles from home. At the end of the tour the battalion was a close knit and proud unit moulded together into a tough fighting force having faced a cunning and resourceful enemy over many months. I was fortunate enough to be decorated, reflecting not just my exploits, but those of my men. Outwardly the often dangerous and deadly experiences we had endured had not touched us mentally because to show one's real emotions was not something one did in a unit such as ours; it would have been seen as a sign of weakness. But I, and others, were deeply touched mentally by our ordeals, although we would never admit to it at the time and I can recall vividly, to this day, all the horrors we went through at a time when all of us had barely left school.

This book will appeal to anybody who picks it up as, from the very first paragraph, it draws you in to a fascinating insight of village life in Dent, Cumbria, between the great wars but focusing primarily on Stan's life as Cavalryman in the 24th Lancers and the Royal Tank Regiment in World War II and his rehabilitation, having suffered horrendous burn injuries and combat stress. The daily routine of a soldier in the field during World War II will surprise many as much of the time was taken up by routine administration and inactivity between engagements with the Germans.

The author is donating the proceeds of the book sales to the 'Help for Heroes' charity, a charity set up to help ex-service men and women who have mental as well as physical injuries as a result of being involved in conflicts around the world. By reading the book you are not only contributing to the charity but also gaining a greater understanding of Post Traumatic Stress, suffered by servicemen and women on the battlefields of today, so vividly portrayed by Stan Haygarth's story.

Governments over the centuries have readily sent soldiers, sailors and more recently airmen to war or lesser conflicts without any real thought for their well being on return home. For example, it is only recently that the Government have dedicated greater resources for the 'aftercare' of servicemen on their return from operational tours. Since the first Gulf War, nearly 20 years ago, the Government have been forced by the general public and media to accept that there is such a condition as Post Traumatic Stress which requires dedicated treatment often over long periods of time.

In the days of Stan Haygarth's service there was very little help for many thousands of men and women who were mentally damaged and, in consequence they had to suffer largely in silence. Many still do today and it is charities such as Help for Heroes and a greater public awareness through stories, such as Stan Haygarth's, exerting pressure on the government of the day that will assure proper treatment for Post Traumatic Stress for those that need it. Sadly too late for Stan Haygarth whose post war years in Sedbergh were bedevilled by illness, both mental and physical suffered during the Normandy landings.

Lieutenant-Colonel Nicholas Emson, M.C.

Acknowledgements

Many thanks to Doris Haygarth for allowing me access to not only personal letters from Stan, but other family letters and archive material that she had kept for nearly 70 years. It was invaluable information and also very moving to read.

Thanks are also due to Leonard Willis, the author of *None had Lances*, the story of the 24th Lancers and to Lieutenant Colonel Nick Emson for the foreword.

This book would not have been possible without Brian Steadman - special thanks to him for his support, encouragement and belief in me.

Carole Morland, 2010

Contents

1
Ada

ADA let out a long sigh as she hauled the heavy wet sheet out of the dolly tub into the rollers of the mangle. It was late morning and she had been hard at work since six o'clock when she had made Fred's breakfast, but it was not tiredness that was making her sigh. Oh no, she was used to hard work; it had been a close companion all of her life and despite her thin, almost bird-like figure she was physically strong.

The daughter of a quarryman from a village near to Barnard Castle in County Durham she had, like many children of her time, been brought up in poverty and on leaving school at thirteen had started work in service. Marriage to Fred Haygarth, the village cobbler in Dent, had brought security in that they owned their own home, but despite the fact that most of the farmers in Dentdale wore clogs or boots that were hand-made by Fred, money was frequently short as Fred was too kind hearted to press them for debts owing for either repairs or new boots. Quite often an outstanding account would be settled by Fred accepting a joint of pork or 'spare rib' from a newly killed pig!

Ada

In addition, since their

marriage, Ada and Fred had four children to care for. Although Fred was a loving father with strict Christian principles on how a family should be raised and who insisted that they should attend the Congregational Chapel at least once, if not twice, every Sunday, it was Ada who bore the brunt of rearing the children. It was she who kept the house clean, who cooked their meals, who knitted and sewed their clothes, who looked after them when they were sick, listened to their woes and who loved them unconditionally.

No, it was something quite different to physical tiredness that was making her sigh. The morning news on the radio was full of the fact that Hitler had disregarded all warnings, had invaded Poland and as a result, Britain was now at war with Germany. Her stomach had churned at this news. Her eldest daughter, Hilda, was a nurse in London and surely, Ada reasoned, London would become a target for Hitler's bombs. Her eldest son John was 22-years-old, and the age when he would surely be called up to serve his country in one of the armed forces. Stanley, her beloved youngest son at only eighteen-years-old, was headstrong, completely naïve and unworldly but had already declared that, "if we are going to war with Germany, I shall be joining up."

Although her life had been hard, up until Hitler started his 'shenanigans' as Ada termed it, she had been happy. Her home was quite large compared to many and she alone kept it spotless. Her 'kitchen' was a stone flagged cellar which was below ground level at the front but opened on to a small garden at the rear. The cellar steps were steep and made of stone and she was up and down them dozens of times in a day. It was here in her cellar that she did the washing and made her bread for the week. The bread was stored in a large earthenware jar at the foot of the cellar steps.

The coal was housed in a recess at the end of the cellar and this had to be carried up the stairs to fuel the large black range which, in addition to heating the living room, housed an oven. A large black kettle was hooked over the open fire and was almost always on the boil. The cellar was 'white washed' but Ada prided herself on her ability to wallpaper and most of the other rooms were papered.

The floor in the living room was covered with linoleum and a large 'clipping' or 'proddy' rug. Making the clipping rugs was a social event as Ada and a group of her friends would gather at each other's houses several evenings a week where they would all sit around a wooden frame over which was stretched washed jute sacking. They would all have hooks with which they would prod strips of material cut up from old clothes, through the mesh of the jute and secure them with a neat knot on the wrong side of the rug. Patterns were created according to the amount of each colour they had. As they worked, they talked incessantly, catching up on the village gossip and discussing what they would be baking for the Harvest Festival or the Christmas Chapel Social. Yes, they were busy, yet happy days, but how long would they last? Not even the smallest villages in the Dales had remained untouched by the 1914-18 War and all of them had lost young men. Would this war be any different?

Ada knew that it was no good appealing to Fred for help in calming her fears for her children. As far as Fred was concerned there were no grey areas in life; everything was in black and white in that you lived your life as a good Christian. In Fred's world this meant being totally fair and honest, attending Chapel every Sunday, not drinking or gambling, not harassing your less well off neighbours for outstanding debts and serving your country in whatever way necessary. Fred himself was very proud of having served in the Staffordshire Regiment in the 1914-18 war. Ada knew that he would expect no less of his sons in this war.

She pegged her sheets on the line in the garden at the rear of the cobbler's shop in Dent's Main Street and before returning to the house paused for a moment to look at the fells that swept up Deepdale and Cowgill. It all looked so normal. It was hard to imagine that another war had started. She felt so angry and cheated; they had promised that the 1914-18 war would be the last and when Fred came home alive she believed that it was the start of a new peaceful world and any children that she and Fred had would not have to know about wars, never mind have to fight in them. Fred had told her bits and pieces about his time fighting in the First World War, but safe in his arms, it had been in the past and had not seemed too real or scary. Now with her own children facing the same prospect, everything that he had told her came flooding back with a new clarity and she felt sick with fear.

2
Fred

FRED'S workshop was accessed from the living room of the house from the side and via three stone steps from the Main Street at the front. The uneven sloping floorboards creaked and the ceiling was low, but there was adequate light from the windows on three sides.

Fred

The first thing that any-one entering the work-shop noticed was the glorious smell of new leather. Several large untouched sheets, of varying thickness, lay in a pile on a table and another sheet from which the shapes of clog 'uppers' had been cut lay on a workbench. The shelves on the walls were filled with wooden clog soles of all sizes, from small chil-dren's to large adult's, metal 'caulkers', tacks, metal boot studs and heels, reels of strong thread and chunks of dark orange coloured wax with which to waterproof the thread.

Fred donned his

leather apron at first light and a large part of his day would be spent sitting under the side window, his 'last' between his knees, painstakingly sewing the 'uppers' to the soles of boots with neat uniform stitches. From time to time a blob of the orange wax would be run along the thread so that the stitching would not rot when the boots got wet. At other times he would have several 'tacks' held between his lips whilst tacking the leather uppers of the clogs to the wooden soles. Behind him on the window ledge was a screw topped jar containing a poisonous adder, 'pickled' in formalin, which had been captured in the village years earlier, and held a gory fascination for the local children!

In winter the workshop was heated by a coke-fuelled stove and the door to the main street was kept closed. On warm summer days however, the open door afforded Fred a wonderful view of the village church with 'Risehill' fell in the background. The local women walking past to one of the two grocer's shops in the village would call out a cheery greeting and he would enjoy seeing the farmers passing with their horse drawn carts to the market town of Sedbergh, some five miles away or the occasional lorry bringing coal from Dent station.

Below the workshop and accessed by a cobblestone slope was the 'stable'. It was windowless with white washed walls and a floor made of the same brown oblong shaped cobble stones as the entrance. Much to his youngest son Stan's disappointment, Fred had never owned a horse and the 'stable' now housed his motorcycle and sidecar, but nevertheless the faint musky smell of hay and horses lingered.

Fred's working days were long; often continuing late into the evening when he worked by lamplight. They were usually fairly solitary days; his work only occasionally interrupted by the odd customer bringing in boots or clogs for repairs and by the infrequent sales representative or traveller as they were known in those days. However, he was happy with his own company and his own thoughts.

He loved the village of Dent with its unique cobblestoned

streets stretching from just above the village school at the south end almost to his shop at the north end and down to Ernie Batty's shop and the Post Office at the east end. But more than the 'chocolate box' prettiness of the village, he loved the fact that the village had a soul. Everyone knew everyone, after all most of them had been born and bred here; they had attended school together, grown up together and continued to both work and socialise together. They had grieved together over the young men of the village lost in the last war and would continue to stand together and support each other through this one.

Although rigid in his Christian beliefs, he was by no means dour or stern; he was kind-hearted with a sense of humour and a twinkle in his eye. He was noted for his fairness and although a quiet man, would readily spring to the aid or defence of anyone that he thought was being treated unfairly or the victim of an injustice. His first reaction to the morning radio news therefore, had been complete outrage, at the injustice to the Polish people of Hitler's latest decision. He had noticed Ada biting her lower lip at the news and seen the troubled expression in her eyes. Whilst he understood and shared her concern for their children, he would not try to deter them from fighting for freedom from tyranny.

3
Stanley

"STOP that this minute Stanley Haygarth or I shall tell your Mother," came the shout from Auntie Dora. Auntie Dora lived in the cottage opposite the Adam Sedgwick Memorial Fountain. This was a large upright block of granite with water running down it into a granite trough below. The trough had an outlet pipe into a drain so the water level in the trough was kept constant. Known locally as 't'fountain' it attracted the local children like a magnet and on this particular day Stan and a couple of his friends were taking turns in blocking up the outlet pipe so that the trough overflowed.

T'fountain at Dent.

Auntie Dora, who felt it her duty to keep a watch on the goings on in the Main Street, had observed Stan crouched next to the fountain with his hand over the outlet pipe. On hearing her shout, Stan reluctantly removed his hand from the outlet pipe and examined the damp sleeve of the jacket that he was rapidly out growing. He thought he would probably be in for a telling off from 'Mam' in any case, as the jacket also had a pungent whiff of pig due to the fact that he and his friends had earlier visited Dinsdale's farm where a pig was being killed and had begged the pig's bladder from Mr. Dinsdale. When inflated and tied with string, pig's bladders made a great, even if a trifle smelly, football!

Keen though she was to observe and report on any mischief that Stan and his pals got up to, she had not noticed

Stanley, aged eleven years.

when they had tied cobbler's thread to the door handles of two houses opposite each other in the Main Street allowing just enough 'slack' for each door to be opened about six inches. They then knocked on each door and watched the ensuing tug-of-war as both householders answered the knock!

Stan, now aged nineteen, smiled at these memories as he leaned on the wall at Church Bridge, staring into the sparkling water where he had often paddled and tickled trout. Looking back it seemed that all his childhood summers had been sunny and nearly all his memories happy. He had no doubt that his elder sisters Mary and Hilda had spoiled him and that he was the apple of Mam's eye. Dad insisted that he do his fair share of chores, like chopping the firewood and delivering repaired boots and clogs to the local farmers and he had had to carry water from 't'fountain' by the bucket for Mam on wash days, but aside from that the school summer holidays had been filled with pleasurable, if at times mischievous, activities.

He loved horses and many pleasant days had been spent leading the heavy horses as they pulled the sleds piled with hay back to the barns at a nearby farm. On some occasions he was even allowed to sit on their backs and steer them, rather than lead them.

Some of his friends were not so lucky. In particular he thought of Harry. Harry had been orphaned and sent to live with his aunt in Dent. The aunt was childless herself and was not happy to have had someone else's child foisted on to her. She begrudged the money to clothe Harry and fed him on as little as possible. Harry often asked Stan and his other pals what they had had for their various evening meals as all of Harry's meals seemed to consist of thin porridge.

Stan and his pals decided that this aunt of Harry's, who was also very house proud, should be taught a lesson and one evening after Harry had been called inside, they captured one of the aunt's hens from her back garden and climbed up on to her roof. They pushed the hen down the chimney, from whence it arrived in the kitchen, via the hearth, with a monstrous squawk and a flurry of soot covered feathers. The soot went everywhere and the aunt was so incandescent with rage that Harry was sent to bed with no supper at all! Stan suffered from guilt for a long time afterwards when Harry recounted what had happened!

Dad insisted that in addition to attending chapel twice on Sunday, the children also attended Sunday School in the afternoon. This was held in the room adjoining the chapel which in winter was heated by a large, black, coke-fuelled stove. Stan and his pals relieved the boredom of the lessons by spitting on the red hot stove when the teacher's back was turned causing the spittle to whizz across the top of the stove with a very satisfying crackle!

He smiled again at the memory of these childish pranks. His school days had been easy as he had excelled at reading and arithmetic, was a neat writer and gifted at drawing. His name was on the school 'Roll of Honour', not once, but twice for gaining scholarships to Skipton Grammar School. However, he had refused to go, partly because he wanted to leave school as soon as possible and partly because he knew that Fred and Ada could not afford to send him there as a boarder. He was lean and athletic and at school sports days had been hard to beat at running and together with brother John had won many tennis doubles matches.

One of the very few bad childhood memories that he had was of the intense pain that he had undergone when he had suffered what the Doctor described as a 'mastoid' in his ear. He had been very ill and Mam had been beside herself with worry. This worried him now as the illness had left him with one perforated ear drum and tomorrow he had an appointment to join the RAF. He hoped that this would not be discovered in the medical examination that he would have to undergo, thereby scuppering his chances of being accepted.

He had told his employer, (a feed merchant for whom he drove a small lorry delivering animal feed to local farms), that he might soon be in the RAF. His employer had accepted this, albeit in a resigned manner but Mam was a different matter altogether. She was already upset that John was serving with the Army in the Middle East and was dead against Stan joining up before he had to. However, Stan had made up his mind, and after one last lingering look over the bridge at the shoals of minnows swimming against the current, he set off for home. Tomorrow and the excitement of the RAF beckoned.

4
"Sorry lad, you had better go home"

FRED'S Austin car chugged around the steep hairpin bends in bottom gear as it ascended the long hill to Dent Station, which had the distinction of being the highest railway station in England. After parking the car in the yard behind the waiting room, they headed for the ticket office where Stan purchased a ticket to Carlisle. Minutes later the train entered the station, metal clanking against metal, steam hissing and sooty-smelling smoke belching. With a, "See you later Dad," and a beaming smile, Stan boarded the train. "Good luck Son," said Fred and headed home.

Back once again at Dent Station, Fred watched the evening sky redden as he waited for Stan's return train from Carlisle. Seeing the expression on his son's face as he alighted from the train, Fred knew that all was not well. Nothing was said until they were both

Dent Station.

22

seated in the car and Fred asked, "What happened?"

"Seems you need both lugs to be working properly to join the RAF and I've only got one," said Stan sullenly.

Fred said, "Perhaps it's for the best lad."

"How can it be for the best? All me mates will be going off ter war and I'm told, 'sorry lad, you'd better go home.' It's not bloody fair, but I aren't finished yet. Perhaps t'Army won't be as bloody fussy," Stan retorted angrily.

Fred decided that this was not the time to reprimand him about his bad language and little further was said on the journey home.

Newly kitted out in the uniform of the Royal Warwickshire Regiment, aged nineteen years and four months.

On this score Stan was right! This time he travelled by bus to Kendal to the Army Recruitment Office. He passed the medical and was told that the Army would be contacting him in due course. Ada received the news with a heavy heart whilst Stan cheerfully waited for his 'papers' to arrive.

These duly arrived a few weeks later. Once again Fred, this time accompanied by Ada, took Stan up the steep winding hill to Dent Station. On this occasion he was heading for Colchester to be 'kitted out' and commence his basic training with the Royal

Warwickshire Regiment. Fred shook his hand, whilst wishing him "Good luck." Ada held him close for a moment and kissed him; holding back her tears. These would be shed later, in plenty, but in the privacy of her bedroom. He looked so young; he had never been away from home before; how would he cope she wondered?

Stanley arrived at Colchester and was 'kitted out' with his uniform, kit bag and basic essentials. He spent many hours being drilled in the art of marching on the barrack square and even more hours polishing his boots! With seven weeks of basic training successfully completed he was transferred to the 24th Lancers, which was an armoured division and soon found himself being sent on a mechanic's course to Stuart and Arden's at Park Royal, Acton, West London. It was a fourteen week course which would not only teach him something about mechanics but would change his life.

5
Doris

"OH Gawd, not again!" thought Dorothy Cagney as the air raid sirens screamed over Acton in West London. She worried constantly about her three children and her husband when they were out. Tonight her eldest daughter Doris had gone to the cinema, but thankfully her husband Jim, her younger daughter Kathleen and her youngest child Alan were all at home. She hoped that Doris would either soon walk through the door or would be safe in an air raid shelter.

Stan was going back to his digs at Park Royal. He and his fellow soldiers had been told that in the event of air raids and blackouts, they were to help any civilians who appeared lost or frightened. The air raid sirens had sounded, London was blacked out and no buses were running, when Stan came across a young woman standing outside the cinema looking slightly lost. He asked her where she was heading. She replied that she had come to the cinema but the film was cancelled due to the air raids and she was now heading towards the bus stop in order to get home. Stan told her that no buses were running and offered to walk her

Doris.

home. She accepted gladly.

On the way they chatted. He explained that he was doing a mechanic's training course at Park Royal whilst she told him that she was a typist at Napier's Aircraft Factory where her Dad also worked as an engineer. When they reached her home, a sliver of moon broke through the clouds. As she smiled and thanked him, he could see that she had beautiful white straight teeth. On the spur of the moment he asked her for a date. They arranged to meet the following afternoon at the zebra crossing in Acton High Street.

As Stan polished his boots the next day he wondered if he had been a trifle hasty; after all he had only glimpsed her teeth! What if the rest of her was ghastly? Doris too was also wondering if agreeing to meet someone that she had never seen, albeit that he was kind-hearted with a nice voice, was rather stupid. However she decided that if a uniformed soldier waiting in Acton High Street looked awful, she would pretend that she was not his 'date' and would keep on walking!

Stan had a terrible moment when standing at the pre-arranged meeting place, a buxom woman with a spotty complexion and considerably older than himself, walked purposefully towards him.

"Oh no," he thought, but at the last minute she veered to the right heading towards the shops. Then he saw her! She was beautiful; slim with shining shoulder-length jet black hair, grey eyes and a smile that showed those straight white teeth. She approached him tentatively with a hand outstretched and the voice that he remembered from the previous evening said, "Stan?"

He took her hand, smiled back and said "Doris." He was in love…

6
A wedding and a waiting...

AFTER that first date, Stan and Doris met at every opportunity. With money being short not many entertainments were available and many evenings were spent talking in a bus shelter at the local park. The London blitz was at its height and on one particular evening the London docks, six miles away, had been bombed and although Acton was blacked out, Stan was able to read a letter from Ada and Fred that he had received that day by the light from the dock land fires!

All too soon Stan's course at Park Royal was completed and he was sent back up north to Catterick. From here it was easier to get back home to Dent when on leave, but more difficult to see Doris, so their letters flowed back and forth with regularity. By this time

Doris in WAAF uniform and Stan now in Lancer's uniform.

he was a tank driver and after Catterick came a spell at Thetford in Norfolk, which was followed by some intensive driving of Valentine tanks on the Whitby Moors during which time he was billeted in the Royal Hotel. However, having been stripped of furniture and carpets, it was not as comfortable an address as it may have sounded!

Whilst Stan was being sent up and down the country to further his tank driving training, Doris decided that she too would like to serve her country and wrote to Stan to tell him that she proposed to join the Women's Air Force. Although Stan had now been away from home for the best part of two years, and in this time had seen a whole lot more of England than he ever thought possible, his upbringing and his roots were still in Dent where women stayed at home cooking, cleaning and looking after their families. They most certainly did not go to war!

Full of indignation, he wrote to Doris, telling her that if she joined the Women's Air Force he wanted nothing more to do with her. Doris, having a mind of her own, joined anyway and sent him a photograph taken in her new uniform after being kitted out at Gloucester! This particular round was certainly won by Doris as they continued to write to each other and on their next joint leave, Stan invited her to Dent to meet Fred and Ada.

Doris's smile won Fred's heart immediately. If Ada had misgivings about a girl who was so unlike any girl in the village that she had previously thought might make Stan a future wife, then she was wise enough to keep them to herself! Doris was amazed at the tranquillity of Dent. It was as if there was no war going on! You could actually get dressed up for an evening out at the local dance hall without hearing an air raid siren or without ending up in the gutter with your hands over your head!

It was therefore with a light heart that she got ready for the Friday night dance at the nearby market town of Sedbergh that Stan was taking her to. The Masonic Hall at Sedbergh was not exactly on a par with the Hammersmith Palais, where most of her dancing skills had been learned, but nevertheless there was a good atmosphere and a passable band so she relished the thought of the evening ahead. Halfway through the evening, Stan asked her to step outside as he wanted to speak to her without shouting over the music. Once outside, he put his arms around her and said, "Will you marry me?"

The wedding.

Doris said, "Yes." Johnstone & Court's jeweller's shop at Kendal was the first stop the next day and an engagement ring was purchased.

Doris was then sent to Morecambe for the next spell of her training. This happened to be only about 35 miles from Dent so Fred and Ada visited her whenever possible and got to know more of their future daughter-in-law.

Stan by this time had been sent to Crowborough in Sussex where his Squadron (C) was inspected by Winston Churchill. After this, a spell at Rottingdean, near Brighton followed. Doris was stationed in Leeds at this time, undergoing her wireless operator's training and it was while she was here that they arranged their wedding.

The wedding took place on 10th May 1942 at St. Peter's Church, Acton. Stan was one month short of his 21st birthday. (His 21st birthday, incidentally, was to be celebrated with a bottle of beer sent to him whilst on guard duty by his Sergeant!)

The wedding was attended by Fred and Ada, Stan's sister Mary, his cousin Lesley, his sister Hilda and her Canadian soldier boyfriend Walter, Doris's parents Dorothy and Jim Cagney, her sister Kathleen, who was bridesmaid and her brother Alan. Walter, the Canadian boyfriend of Hilda, had to step in at the last minute as best man because Stan's Fitter Sergeant, who was the designated best man, failed to turn up! He had been posted elsewhere the day before and had been unable to let them know! After the reception, Stan and Doris spent a weekend's honeymoon at her aunt's house in Richmond, Surrey.

The wedding had provided a pleasant interlude but Stan was continually wondering what all this training was about and asking himself when he was going to actually see some action? He had joined up to fight Hitler and so far he had not done any fighting! He did not want to spend the whole damned war being trained!

However, his next posting to Bovington, for further tank training, was simultaneous with Doris's posting to Compton Bassett in Wiltshire so they were not too far apart and able to see each other when their respective leaves coincided. Several months passed with Doris being transferred to Bournemouth where her service career ended on discovering her pregnancy. Stan received the news in a letter with mixed feelings. On the one hand he would no longer have to worry about Doris being posted abroad; he felt sure that his Mam and Dad would welcome her to stay in the comparative safety of Dent. On the other hand, he was going to be a father! What did the future hold for a baby?

His baby daughter was born on the 3rd May 1944 and Stan was given a few days of compassionate leave to see her and Doris. Once his leave was over, his final training took place at Chippenham in Wiltshire. He had previously driven Valentine and

Crusader tanks, but it was here that he not only drove his first Sherman tank but also practiced loading it onto a Tank Landing Craft.

Towards the end of May it was obvious that something momentous was about to happen. Postal censorship was introduced so Stan could no longer say in his letters home where he was. Generals Montgomery and Eisenhower gave them 'pep' talks and told them they were about to invade the enemy stronghold. The last day of May saw their tanks rolling slowly along in convoy, flanked by Military Police towards the docks of Southampton and London. The waiting was over...

Through the mud and the blood...

D DAY - the 6th June dawned and they were on their way through the grey choppy waters of the English Channel. As far as Stan could see there were ships of all shapes and sizes whilst overhead the RAF Bombers buzzed constantly. He was on what was called a Landing Ship (Tank) which was a large vessel that carried tanks and other vehicles on two decks. Huge doors opened in the bows from which the tanks drove down a ramp.

As they drew nearer to the beach code named 'Gold' it became obvious that all was not going well. The beach was littered with tanks, bulldozers and landing craft that were all out of action. Stretcher bearers were rushing about with wounded men but the sight that made Stan's blood run cold was that of the tops of lorries, bulldozers and tanks sticking out of the water. They had not made it ashore.

Because it was not thought possible for the Landing Ships to get near enough to the shore for the tanks to just drive down the ramps on to the beaches, powered rafts, known as 'Rhinos', had been designed to take the tanks the last 600 yards to land. However, it was not possible to steer these Rhinos, and thus they were not proving entirely effective. The only other option was for the Landing Ships to actually go in as far as possible and just let the tanks roll off through the bow doors. All this took far longer than anticipated and it was D Day plus one (7th June) when Stan was finally in the

Gold Beach

seat of his tank and ready to roll off the ship.

Never having learned to swim because of his perforated eardrum, he had a considerable fear of water and as he prepared to drive ashore he prayed that he would not drown before he even arrived in Normandy. His relief on emerging from the sea on to the central (Jig Green) part of Gold Beach was immense even though it was apparent from the noise, smoke, dead bodies and utter confusion that they had entered a hell that no training on earth could have prepared them for.

The Allies had planned to take Caen, one of the largest cities in Normandy and a vital German defensive position, on D Day. However, this did not happen and the battle for Caen was to last throughout June, July and August. It was 11pm on the 7th June by the time all of the 24th Lancer's tanks were ashore, assembled and had their waterproofing removed. Orders came at 7am on 8th June to concentrate on Martragny, a village just north of the Bayeaux-Caen main route and from here to advance to Putot-en-Bessin which is halfway between Bayeux and Caen. This was Stan's first taste of real action.

German Panzers had already driven Canadian troops out of Putot, and despite artillery support the Lancers were given a hard time by German anti-tank guns and three battalions of a Panzer Grenadier Regiment. The Lancers knocked out two self propelled guns and two anti-tank guns. There were many German casualties (both wounded and killed) and 75 German prisoners were taken. The Lancers lost six men with others wounded. At this point it was hard to ascertain Stan's feelings as his first letter to Doris from Normandy (obviously mindful of censorship) made no mention of battle and merely told her, "not to worry as he was taking good care of himself!"

After an evening back at Martragny, to refuel the tanks and reload with ammunition, 9th June saw the Regiment advance to Point 103, which overlooked the occupied town of Tilly-sur-Seulles. All day they were under heavy fire and surrounded by German tanks but later in the day, together with the Durham Light

Infantry, they successfully captured St. Pierre and Stan's C Squadron remained there overnight to help the infantry hold and secure the bridge leading to Tilly-sur-Seulles.

June 10th saw the Germans again attack St. Pierre but despite C Squadron losing four members, St. Pierre was held. The next day saw another battle for St. Pierre and it was held again despite the Lancers losing six tanks. The next day, June 12th, was one of the Lancer's worst days as fifteen men were wounded and ten killed. The 13th June saw similar fighting and on the 14th June C Squadron withdrew their tanks to the rear of Point 103 while the RAF bombed Tilly-sur-Seulles.

This was Stan's first rest break after almost seven days of continuous fighting. He wrote to Doris, "If you had seen me last night you would hardly have recognised me; I looked like a scarecrow! I had not had a wash or a shower for four days and was I black! I am sure I have got blisters on my bottom for I have only been out of my tank seat for ten hours out of the last eighty. Last night though I slept outside and I had a good seven hours sleep and some breakfast this morning."

That day continued relatively easily with only tank maintenance, refuelling and reloading with ammunition to see to but the next day, June 16th, saw Stan in action again supporting the King's Own Yorkshire Light Infantry in an attack on the village of Cristot. This attack was successful and C Squadron was able to rest until late evening of the next day (June 17th) when they were sent to Parc de Bois Londe, a wood South of Cristot, to relieve B Squadron, who had gained and held this position earlier in the day.

June 18th was Stan's 23rd birthday, and in the late morning C Squadron was relieved by the Sherwood Rangers Yeomanry allowing Stan and his tank crew to enjoy a few extra cigarettes that his eldest sister, Hilda, had sent for his birthday! It should probably be explained at this point that the daily 'free' ration for each soldier was seven cigarettes, one small chocolate bar and five boiled sweets so any soldier who smoked more than seven a day relied on either parcels from home or exchanging chocolate bars and boiled sweets with the non-smokers for their extra ones!

Operation 'Epsom', a further attack on Caen was being planned, and the first stage of this involved a set piece attack on Tessel Wood. This had been due to start on June 19th but Normandy was attacked by a greater force than either Germany or England could muster; the weather! The worst summer storm for forty years lashed the area, holding up shipping and thus supplies.

During the week that the storm lasted, the troops were able to catch up on their washing and letter writing. They were also able to better acquaint themselves with what was on offer in the Normandy countryside as Stan recounts that the fresh eggs 'pilfered' from the Normandy hen houses were much superior to the dried egg in their rations! They were also able to hone their

Sherman Tank of 24th Lancers.

culinary 'skills' as Stan wrote, "Today I bashed our hard biscuits to powder with a hammer and mixed the resulting powder with tinned sardines and made fish cakes. For 'afters' we had stewed apple. We picked them from a nearby orchard and sweetened them with our boiled sweet ration."

The tanks rolled out of camp after midnight on the 25th June crossing the river at Bas de Fontenay en route for Tessel Wood. A huge artillery barrage preceded the infantry who were supported by strong machine gun fire from B Squadron on the left and C Squadron on the right. The enemy responded with heavy and intense mortar fire and casualties on both sides were heavy. By nightfall the infantry had gained control of part of Tessel Wood and C Squadron had orders to remain there overnight to reinforce this. After this particular battle Stan had a huge respect for the infantry and wrote home, "The infantry really think we are Gods or something and they will do anything so long as the tanks are there. Believe me our infantry are the bravest lads I have ever seen. I have seen some very brave deeds done and they don't even think anything of it. If the people back home could see it all they would really salute these soldiers."

However, not all of the people of Normandy saluted these soldiers; in the confusion of war, there were some reports of women spitting on soldiers in the towns and villages. Mostly though, they were warmly welcomed; with, in some cases, bottles of wine that had been successfully hidden from the Germans. The candy and chocolate bars that the American forces had in profusion, brought smiles to the faces of the children of Normandy, many of whom were tasting them for the first time.

The next two days saw C Squadron continuing to guard the west side of Tessel Wood until moving on the 29th June to Les Hauts Vents, from where they continued on the 30th June to Rauray to relieve the 4th/7th Royal Dragoon Guards. On 1st July, reports were received that some seventy German tanks were amassed ready to attack Rauray, and at dawn the first attack took place, with C Squadron bearing the main force of the attack. Fighting was

as our pin up girl and told me to make sure that I got her photo out of the tank when we moved to the Royal Tank Regiment!" It should be mentioned at this point that the official motto of the Royal Tank Regiment is "Fear Naught," but the unofficial (and perhaps more apt) motto is, "Through the mud and the blood to the green fields beyond," which inspired the titles of two chapters of this book.

After his transfer to the Royal Tank Regiment Stan writes home, "we are miles behind the enemy lines now but the food is better and note the change of address! It now has B.L.A. added which means British Liberation Army - they don't half give us some fancy titles!" The 3rd of August is Doris's 21st Birthday and Stan sends her an extra £5 saved from his pay and tells her "not to worry as he is looking after himself, but he wishes that he could be back home to celebrate her birthday". Little does he know that the bloodiest and most awful battle of the Normandy campaign is fast approaching...

On the 12th August, Stan wrote home, "It is almost too hot to eat but today we had tinned meat, veg and potatoes and for afters we made pancakes." It is almost impossible to comprehend that, possibly due to censorship of their letters home and more probably to ease their loved one's worries, soldiers would write about what they had to eat on the eve of one of the bloodiest battles in history!

By the 13th August the Battle of Falaise or Falaise Pocket was underway. Whole books have been written about this battle alone but basically huge numbers of German soldiers were encircled by the allies with only one route out, hence the term 'pocket'. This route was then blocked resulting in 10,000 Germans being killed and 50,000 being taken prisoner. The fighting was desperate, a number of German units escaped but simultaneous air strikes and massed artillery attacks did a vast amount of damage to those who had not escaped. The Falaise 'pocket' was filled with burned out tanks, dead German horses and most horrifyingly dead and injured men.

On the 20th Anniversary of Falaise, General Eisenhower commented, "No other battlefield presented such a horrible sight of death, hell and total destruction."

Stan wrote, "I have seen lorry loads of German prisoners going to the 'cages' – they looked browned off." He also must have been feeling battle fatigued and horrified by the sights as he wrote, "I was feeling very homesick today. When I come home, just throw your arms around me and hold me close for a week and make me forget what I have seen here. If you and I and baby can have a little cottage somewhere peaceful, I shall not ever want anything more." But ever the comic, he adds, "but never cook me stew please, we get it every day and all I can think about is eating bread!"

By the 22nd August, the Battle of Falaise is over and on the 23rd August, the tanks of the Royal Tank Regiment (RTR) enter the Cathedral city of Lisieux. German machine gun resistance is unexpectedly high and another bloody battle ensues but by the 25th August, Lisieux is liberated. The famous Basilica, which housed the remains of St. Therese, and in which the towns people of Lisieux took refuge during the battle, amazingly remained intact despite the bombing and the vicious street fighting.

Ironically, Lisieux is reported as the last 'real' battle of Normandy as most of the German forces were by now in retreat, intent on reaching Paris to cross the River Seine. The task of Stan and his crew, along with other tanks of the Royal Tank Regiment was to keep pushing them towards this. Whilst passing through a wooded area near Elbeuf, south of Rouen, on the 27th August, they encountered 'Tigers' in the woods. Not the orange striped variety but German Tiger tanks. These tanks were hidden amongst the trees to the sides of the woodland track along which the RTR tanks were travelling. As Stan was later to recount, "we were sitting ducks."

A shell hit the rear section of their tank. The noise and vibration was tremendous with flames appearing almost simultaneously. Stan looked across to Phil, his co-driver, who had opened his hatch, (which was the only route out for both of them as Stan's was jammed), but Phil was not getting out.

"For Christ's sake Phil, get out, I'm on fire," shouted Stan. Phil replied, "I can't, my leg is stuck." After what seemed an eternity, Phil finally struggled free and exited the tank via the hatch. Stan followed, and once out of the hatch, rolled down from the tank to the ground. It was only when he was on the ground, and conscious of the machine gun fire aimed at him, that he realised that he could not use his hands to crawl along the ground. There was no skin left on either of them; he was looking at two blackened clumps of raw flesh. However, the will to live was great and he proceeded to crawl, using his elbows rather than his hands, keeping below the machine gun fire to summon help for the rest of the crew.

One of two reports in English newspapers said:

"L. Cpl. Stanley Haygarth, of the Royal Tank Regiment, has been wounded during operations near Rouen in France. He was trapped in his tank when the ammunition box became ablaze. Although suffering from severe burns, L. Cpl. Haygarth managed to get out of the tank and under heavy machine gun fire crawled to get assistance for the tank crew. He was taken to a base hospital where he received treatment and was recently transferred to a hospital in England.

"He is the younger son of Mr and Mrs Fred Haygarth of Main Street, Dent. He is 23 years of age. He is married and has a daughter aged four months. Along with his mother, his wife and daughter visited him in hospital and although he is still very ill is reported to be making satisfactory progress."

Stan's war in Normandy ended here, but his own personal war was just beginning.

... to the green fields beyond

"AH'M reet sorry lass, but I've a telegram for thee from t'War Office. Ah 'ope it's not reet bad news aboot yer 'usband," said the postman as he handed Doris the thin brown envelope. Prior to the war the postman had enjoyed his job. He knew all the families in Dent village and the surrounding dales and it pained him to have to be the one to deliver the dreaded brown envelopes from the War Office to these families whose sons were serving in the Forces.

Doris had been living with Fred and Ada since a couple of months after her baby daughter Carole had been born on the 3rd May 1944. It was now September. Stan had been in Normandy since June. With a shaking hand Doris took the envelope, opened it and read the contents. Looking at Fred and Ada's anxious white faces she quickly reassured them that the telegram stated that Stan was wounded, not dead. Ada, practical as always, brewed a cup of tea and they decided that Doris should go round to the Post Office and send off telegrams to inform the rest of the family of the news.

The Post Office was manned by Aunt Gita, the wife of one of Fred's brothers, who did not know what to make of Doris with her London accent, who had shocked the female population of the village by wearing trousers of all things! Even Ada had been horrified when Doris appeared one morning in her Women's Auxiliary Air Force (WAAF) issue trousers to take Carole for a stroll in her pram.

"Women folk in Dent don't wear trousers, dear," said Ada.

"They are warm and comfortable and my stockings are full of holes so I intend to wear them," said Doris. Ada decided that perhaps she had a point so said nothing more on the matter although she was well aware that it would cause a stir in the village. When Aunt Gita read the content of the telegram, she murmured her condolences but Doris knew that as soon as she left the Post Office, word would be spread around Dent quicker than a bush fire! Doris walked very slowly back from the Post Office; a multitude of questions chasing round in her head. What did wounded mean? How bad were the wounds? The telegram was dated 7th September and it stated that he had been wounded on the 27th August; where had he been since then and where was he now?

Doris's family and Stan's sisters Mary and Hilda were shocked to receive their telegrams but when John, Stan's brother, who was serving with the 'Desert Rats' in Egypt, received his, it was merely confirmation of what he already knew in his heart. John had a strange gift of telepathy and had said to his Army mates several days earlier that he had a strong feeling that something had happened to his brother, Stan.

Meanwhile, Stan looked around at what appeared to him to be a large tent. A nurse was by his bed, he was aware of severe pain in his hands and head, and of a strange smell. He asked the nurse where he was and what the smell was. The nurse explained that he was in a field hospital in Rouen in France and the smell was coming from the sulphur candles that were being burned in order to try to mask the smell of burnt flesh! She explained that he had been brought there after his tank had been blown up.

The heavy bandages on his head and face soaked up the silent tears that he shed on learning that although Phil, his co-driver was alive, the gunner, the wireless operator and the tank commander, who had all been in the rear part of the tank, which had sustained the brunt of the hit, were dead. With hands also encased in bandages the size of boxing gloves, he had to be fed, washed and sat on a bed pan like a baby. The daily ritual of changing the dressings brought pain beyond belief as the burned flesh fell away. He was told that his family had been informed that he had been wounded.

A few days after receiving the news from the War Office that Stan had been wounded, Doris received another letter from France written in unfamiliar hand writing. It was from an Army Welfare Officer, who explained that he was writing for Stan, who was unable to write himself due to the burns on his hands. It went on to say that Stan was being well cared for and would be brought back to England as soon as possible.

Fourteen days later, on the 21st September, another letter arrived, this time written by an Army Padre, to say that Stan would be coming back to England the following week. The next communication was a postcard dated 28th September from the 'Red Cross & St. John War Organisation - Wounded and Missing Relatives Dept.' This stated that, "5122337 Haygarth has been admitted to Nottingham General Hospital. Owing to the difficulties of travelling and billeting, relatives should not visit unless officially requested to do so by the Hospital Authorities." It went on to say that, "Sister is quite satisfied there is no facial disfigurement." It was signed by Barbara Slater (Liaison Officer) who added that she would write for him.

Ada's reaction to the instruction "not to visit" was to immediately make plans for her, Doris and baby Carole to visit! Fred waved them off at Dent Station, from where they would travel to Nottingham and stay at a boarding house whilst they paid Stan a visit. Stan meanwhile had not been allowed out of bed, much less allowed to look in a mirror, so it was with a mixture of shock, disbelief and horror that he watched his wife holding their baby daughter in her arms, accompanied by his mother, enter the ward, look at him without recognition, then proceed to carry on walking past his bed.

He was too choked with emotion to call out to them and so it was only when the Ward Sister re-directed them to his bedside that they were reunited. Only the baby did not cry. As she gazed at Stan with solemn brown eyes that had not been able to focus the last time he saw her, Stan thought that here was a person who would not grieve over his disfigurement, as she had not known him any other way.

All too soon the visit was over. Ada, Doris and Carole returned to Dent. On the 10th October Stan received an unusual letter, which perhaps epitomised the spirit of the people of Britain at this time. The letter was from a man whose own son had been in the Royal Tank Regiment and had been killed. This is the letter:

Dear Stanley,

You have never heard of me but, the Matron having kindly told me that you have arrived in Nottingham, I thought a note maybe would pass a moment or two for you. I have asked if my wife and I may come and see you when your relatives (if you have any near enough) have been allowed to come. My son was in C Squadron of your Regiment and my wife and I will be glad to do anything we can to help pass the time of any 1st R.T.R. fellows who, like you, have been unfortunate enough to reach the hospital wounded. If when you are allowed out, you may care to come and see us, our home is not far away from the hospital. When you are able to write, perhaps you would like to pass a few minutes by writing to me. With very best wishes for a speedy recovery,

Yours sincerely, Jack Ley.

On the 25th October, Stan wrote that Mr and Mrs Ley have visited him and that he is due to be moved to Harlow Wood Orthopedic Hospital at Mansfield in Nottinghamshire.

His burns are healing to some extent by this stage. The facial skin is re-growing, albeit rather shiny and red. There is nothing much left of his upper ears and he is told that nothing can be done to rebuild them. His hair is growing again and the shrapnel wound on the back of his head has healed. His hands are the worst problem, the right one being worse than the left. The first of many skin grafts had taken place with skin taken from his leg being grafted onto his left hand and he wrote home that both the hand and the leg are healing well. (The letters at this stage are a mixture of those written for him by nurses, and others obviously written with difficulty using only the thumb and index finger of the right hand.)

Fred had been horrified that Ada and Doris had not recognised Stan when they visited him and was sure that he would recognise him. It was therefore a huge shock to Fred when exactly the same happened to him when he visited in early November 1944. Stan wrote to Doris, "It was grand seeing Dad at the weekend but he looked straight at me and didn't know me. Poor Dad, he was upset at first. He said that he was very proud of me."

This letter was addressed to Doris at her parent's new home in Ashford, Middlesex, to where they had recently moved from Acton, West London and where she and the baby were to stay until after the war, despite Stan's worries about the bombs.

By the middle of November Stan wrote that at last he was allowed out of bed through the day and was "helping the nurses." He also wrote of the entertainment that was put on for the injured troops, both in and out of the hospital. He had been allowed to go to the cinema (including a free tea) and the hospital had been visited by a brass band. Also, a man brought along his young daughter who Stan guessed was about ten-years-old, to sing for them. He said that she had the voice of an angel and her name was Petula Clark. Yes, it was the same Petula Clark who went on to become a household name and make many hit records!

Although patients such as Stan were allowed out on supervised trips to the cinema and for tea, they were certainly not allowed out to the 'pub'. Stan and two more soldiers that he had become friendly with declared that they would give anything for a pint of beer. The more they discussed it, the more they longed for it. Stan and another of the three were both mobile, but the third member had lost both of his legs, so this presented something of a problem. Whilst they were discussing a possible solution to this, the hospital gardener came past the ward window pushing his wheelbarrow. Problem solved! Suffice to say that when the evening meal was delivered to the ward, three of its patients were missing, but even though the beer tasted wonderful, the 'dressing down' that Matron administered was enough to ensure that the 'outing' was not repeated!

Stan was declared convalescent just before Christmas which enabled him to spend a week's leave with Doris and the baby at her parent's home in Ashford, Middlesex. He returned to Mansfield after Christmas with life continuing much the same, with Doris visiting whenever she was able to, until the 14th February 1945 when he was transferred to Queen Mary's Hospital, Roehampton, London. Queen Mary's was to be his home for the next eighteen months, although after April 1945 he was allowed home to Doris's parent's house almost every weekend, which gave him a chance to get to know his daughter who, at almost a year old was walking and talking, and who he had so far only had contact with during hospital visits. During this time he had had many more skin graft operations plus two amputation operations; the first being to remove two fingers from the right hand and the second to remove the little finger of the left hand from the knuckle joint.

Stan's discharge from the Army was dated the 31st July 1945 and it states that his Military Record was "Exemplary." On the 30th August 1945 he was invited to attend a Garden Party at Buckingham Palace with other wounded ex-servicemen from Queen Mary's Hospital. The invitation stated that there would be tea, music by the band of the Grenadier Guards and a full supporting musical programme.

However, it was not until autumn 1946, a full two years after he was wounded in Normandy, that Stan is finally discharged from hospital. He and Doris decide that their future home was to be in the north of England and return to Dent.

Stan found Dent to be much the same as it had been before he joined the Army. Crystal water still bubbled down the front of t'fountain into the granite trough below, children wearing clogs his Dad had made still clattered over the cobblestones to school each day and women folk still made 'clipping' rugs whilst talking about what they should bake for the Chapel Harvest Festival or Christmas Social.

It was the very 'normality' of daily life that was so hard to bear when every time that he closed his eyes he could see, hear and smell Normandy. The job that he had had, prior to joining up, as a lorry driver for a local feed merchant, was still there for him as soon as his hands were healed enough to drive, so to pass the time away he had recently gone as a passenger with another driver for

Doris celebrated their Golden Wedding Anniversary surrounded by children, grandchildren and friends. However, Post Traumatic Stress had still not been diagnosed, therefore he never received the help and counselling that he and others like him needed and deserved so he was never able to entirely escape from his personal demons. Even during his last days in hospital, prior to his death, he was again transported mentally to Normandy, re-living it nightly in ghastly dreams. The British Army trained him to fight in a war, but could neither prepare his mind for, nor release it from, the horrors of that war.

Stan died on the 17th October 1997 aged 76 years, at last getting through the mud and the blood to reach those green fields beyond...

The Present

THE landing beaches in Normandy are no longer littered with tanks, bulldozers and landing craft. There is no gun fire or droning overhead bombers. The only sounds are of the waves, which long since washed away the blood, lapping the clean golden sand, the occasional cries of sea birds and the voices of picnicking families enjoying the freedom that is rightfully theirs.

The gaps in the tall green hedges of the *bocage* country of Normandy, made by the cutting instruments attached to the front of American tanks, have long grown together and the lush fields, once littered with the corpses of dead animals are again p e a c e f u l l y grazed. There are no more 'tigers' in the woods, only birds singing joyfully.

Towns, cities and villages are now rebuilt and restored to their former glory.

A casket, containing the remains of St. Therese was brought in September 2009

Caen, Normandy, in 2009.

from the Cathedral of Lisieux to the north of England, where crowds of staunch Catholics queued patiently to touch and kiss it.

If my descriptions of the battles that took place in Normandy in 1944 have not conveyed to the reader the enormity of the bloodshed, then a stroll today through the many well kept cemeteries in the region surely will. No normal person can view the last resting places of 5002 Canadian, 19,709 British, 13,796 American, 696 Polish, 19 French and 58,412 German servicemen without feeling very emotional, humble and grateful.

Doris continues to live independently but surrounded by family, including five great-grandchildren who Stan never met. The smile, showing those teeth, that Stan first fell in love with is still there. The black hair is now white, the eye sight is diminished but the spirit is not, as she fought and defeated cancer in 2007.

Dent has changed. Fred's cobbler's shop is now part of a private house. The banks, the gentlemen's outfitters shop, the butcher's shop and the 'smithy' have long since closed. The Congregational Chapel where Fred and Ada once worshiped, and

Gold Beach, 2009.

War graves in a Normandy cemetery.

in the grounds of which they are buried, has been stripped of its pews and altar and is now a Meditation Centre. The Adam Sedgwick Memorial, otherwise known by those born and bred in Dent as 't'fountain', still trickles water down the large upright stone into the granite trough below. It may well still be a magnet for the local children, but they no longer carry buckets of water home from it on wash day as Stan did, and it is better known these days as a tourist attraction.

The year 2009 was the 70th Anniversary of the start of World War II. Fewer veterans visited Normandy as, like Stan, many of them have now reached "those green fields beyond." Dame Vera Lynn's album of war time songs entitled *We'll Meet Again* amazingly topped the charts!

In 1945 Post Traumatic Stress Syndrome had not been diagnosed, but now that it has, and its severe effects are known, why are increasing numbers of ex-service personnel, battle weary and traumatised, ending up in prison or homeless after turning to alcohol or drugs to blot out their horrific wartime memories? Why, in

2009, on any night of the year are there 1,100 ex-service men and women sleeping rough in London alone? Why is more money per day allocated to feed a criminal in prison than a person in the Armed Forces?

It is reported that soldiers as young as nineteen are being sent to Afghanistan in 2009 after only six weeks battle training. Quite often British soldiers are still not welcomed in the countries that they are sent to liberate, so nothing has changed since Rudyard Kipling wrote (when British soldiers were known as 'Tommies'):

Tommy here and Tommy there and chuck him out the brute,
But it's 'Saviour of his Country' when the guns begin to shoot.

This is no way to treat the 'Saviours of our Country' and is the reason that I chose to tell Stan's story. He was just an ordinary man from an ordinary village, yet he, and many like him, made and continue to make, a difference to this world that we live in.

****

Any profits from the sale of this book will go to the charity 'Help for Heroes,' in memory of Stan and others like him.

Carole Morland has written a book about the fell ponies she knows and loves so well. This book is also published by Hayloft:

A Walk on the Wild Side